MEL BAY PRESENTS

the spirit of
WORLD DRUMMING

jeff stewart

Edited by Anna Stewart
Cover Design by Ron Beltrame
Photography by Will Morin

DRUM CIRCLE FUN FOR ALL AGES

 chapters

1	Getting Started Playing Our Hand Drum	7	Have Fun Playing Auxiliary Percussion Instruments
2	Getting Started Playing Our Hand Drum	8	Empowerment of an Improvisational Drum Circle
3	Getting Started Playing Our Hand Drum	9	Rhythm Studies, Reading Music
4	Rhythm Studies, Reading Music	10	Three Part Rhythm Drum Circle Fun!
5	More Hand Drumming Techniques	11	Experience the Spirit of World Music
6	The Four Essential Rudiments		

1 2 3 4 5 6 7 8 9 0

Visit us on the Web at www.melbay.com — E-mail us at email@melbay.com

TABLE OF CONTENTS

Please view DVD Chapter 8 to experience the empowerment of an
Improvisational Drum Circle that involves community participants of all ages.

INTRODUCTION

This book is a spirited global tour of drum circle instruction for the classroom and community that includes a comprehensive DVD showcasing school and community drum circles. People who want to discover their life sustaining need to drum are welcome to let me take them on a journey of WORLD MUSIC. My book begins with the African forms of drumming and moves through diverse cultural forms of music/drumming from all around our world (African, Cuban, Brazilian, Native, Middle Eastern, Japanese, Community). The instructional DVD showcases the talent of people of all ages. You can refer to the DVD for all the topics covered in the book. This book also provides educators and drum circle facilitators with ideas for implementing a music program or starting a community Drum Circle. I have also included positive evaluation methods for the classroom.

PRACTICE ADVICE TO MEET SUCCESS + ENJOYMENT

I stress the importance of practicing at slow tempos using a metronome or a drum machine. Focus your attention on staying totally relaxed both physically and mentally. Any stress or the tightening of muscles will get in the way of playing your drum(s). Practicing at slow tempos allows you to stay relaxed and focus on further developing your drum techniques. Once you feel confident at playing the music then you can begin practicing at various tempos. It is also very important to listen and play along with recordings of WORLD MUSIC. Purchase a good set of headphones so that you can easily hear and control the volume of the recorded music for accompaniment. Join a community drum circle so you can use your new skills and have fun playing in a group.

SUGGESTIONS ON HOW TO BEGIN A DRUM CIRCLE

If you are interested in forming a drum circle, advertise by putting bulletins in your local music stores or in your newspapers. If you're a teacher, educator or a student, access your groups internet bulletin board and advertise a drum circle gathering. Find a location, set a date, a time of gathering and keep it the same day on a weekly or bi-weekly basis. Schedule your drum circle gatherings from 4 to 6 sessions. With the approval of the city/community in which you live, plan to meet at a park (weather permitting) for a drum circle gathering.

A FREQUENTLY ASKED QUESTION
MY JOB AS A DRUM CIRCLE FACILITATOR

I am asked this question on a regular basis when I am facilitating drum circles …
"Do I have to have any musical training or talent to participate in a Drum Circle?" My response is, "No! You don't have to have any musical background to participate in my Drum Circles." It is my job as a drum facilitator to bring out your primitive understanding of rhythm and beat. Everyone has a heartbeat and a sense of rhythm. The important element is the person's keen interest in participating.

If you are looking to have your drum circle perform in the community, do not be shy! Check the entertainment section of your newspapers, or community internet sites for music/art festivals that you can approach about performing. Make sure that they are aware of the interest that your community drum circle has in performing at their function. Spread the great SPIRIT of DRUMMING.

I wish you all the best. Do not hesitate. Participate and spiritually enjoy playing your drum(s).
Discover your Spirit of Drumming.

SPIRITUAL REFLECTION

I am a very thankful kidney recipient. A donor from my Ontario community gave me and my family this wonderful life sustaining gift back in the year 2000. Thanks to my donor and their family.

WHOLE PERSON THERAPY

In December of 2003, I suddenly became very ill. In February of 2004 I was flown to London, Ontario. From January to Easter I still do not remember the struggles and the operation on my brain. The doctors (a team of more than 10) consulted and decided brain surgery was needed for a diagnosis of a cyst growing in my brain. For the operation, they had to remove a small piece of bone from the left side of my skull, a reminder I will have for life of my illness. Not to worry though, this illness is very rare. I want to thank our outstanding Canadian health care system. We are very lucky to be Canadian.

It was a traumatic event to be forced out of my loving Sudbury community. I felt lost, confused, helpless and scattered. I came to feel like I had become a different person. I did not know who I was and continued to always question myself. The first memory that I had after my operation occurred at Easter and it was when I took my first steps to a new life. Thanks to Tom for helping me take my first steps, to Denise my devoted physiotherapist at the London University Hospital and my loving wife Anna who patiently continued to help me regain my health. I remember asking Denise and my wife when I would be able to practice walking up and down the stairs. I was determined to prepare myself for my return to my love of teaching, and the school where I work has three flights of stairs. Why was I concerned with walking the stairs, when my first focus should have been to relearn to walk? Now that I reflect on this, I felt lost. Who was I? Jeff? I did not feel like a whole person.

RHYTHM OF REHAB

Towards the spring of 2004, I was finally transferred back to my home community of Sudbury to Laurentian Rehab centre. My loving community organized a fundraising concert for my benefit. I was not well enough to attend. I want to take this moment to thank everyone who attended, organized and performed at my benefit concert. Thank you to my family and friends especially Joey Adetuyi for being my closest friend and a spiritual brother.

This period of rehab was very difficult and confusing. There were many times when I had breakdowns and disagreements with my therapists. My motor skills, memory and speech were very slow. This was a period of confusion. My therapists were devoted in helping me become a whole person again. Sue, who was my recreation therapist, had the key to open the proper door for me to become a whole person; she recognized the love I have for teaching and playing music. She encouraged me to have my wife bring in not just one drum but two so that I could play and by teaching Sue to play to rediscover my love of drumming and music. Playing and teaching my doumbek drum helped me to get organized and to foster my sequencing skills. It helped me get into the rhythm of rehab. Drumming "grounded me". Sue set up a room in the rehab center where I could practice drumming. Every night with the encouragement of my nurses, I practiced for 2 to 3 hours. After three weeks of drumming and teaching Sue, my therapists, doctors, family and friends noticed a big improvement in my capabilities. I felt that I had become a whole person again. Before I was released from the centre, my speech language pathologist Catherine had each patient choose a topic to prepare for a presentation. My topic was drum circle. Drumming was my spiritual rejuvenation experience. I have personally experienced the health benefits of letting my DRUMS heal my physical and spiritual being. Drumming has helped me look at life and how I can give back to my community in a positive way. I have come to realize my love of facilitating drum circles in my community. I think of the entire World as my community.

If you feel down or you're suffering from any health related problems, pick up your drum, close your eyes and spiritually let your heart lead you to play your drum(s). Let go and let your natural sense of rhythm come out from you to create a joyful/spiritual musical environment for yourself. Experiment with textures, tempo(s) and playing techniques.

CHAPTER 1

GETTING STARTED PLAYING OUR HAND DRUM

WHAT IS A DJEMBE?
WHERE DOES THE DJEMBE COME FROM?

A Djembe (pronounced JEM-bay) also known as djimbe, jenbe, jembe, yembe or sanbanyi in Susu; is a skin covered hand drum, shaped like a large goblet, and meant to be played with bare hands. It is a member of the membranophone family of musical instruments: a frame or shell (in the djembe's case it is a shell) covered by a membrane or drumhead made of one of many products, usually rawhide. The djembe originated in West Africa, and is an integral part of the region's musical tradition and culture. The djembe is now popular all over the world.

A masterful djembe player may be referred to as a "djembefola" - "the one who makes the djembe speak."

Djembe - Wikipedia, the free encyclopedia: en.wikipedia.org

AFRICAN NOTATION
LET'S PLAY SOME DRUMS AND HAVE FUN

African Hand Drumming Tones

Bass Tones

Goon = Right Hand (B)

Doon = Left Hand (B)

Open Tones

Goe = Right Hand (O)

Doe = Left Hand (O)

Slap Tones

Pah = Right Hand (S)

Tah = Left Hand (S)

Heel / Toe Tones

Heel = Palm of Hand (H)

Toe = Fingers of Hand (T)

AFRICAN HAND DRUM PLAYING TECHNIQUES

Begin by shaping your hands into a triangle over the drum head. The triangle will be created in the space between your thumbs and index fingers.

The **Bass Tones** are performed by tapping the middle of the hand drum. Remember to let your hands rebound off the drum head (like bouncing a basketball). Play the drum with the palms and fingers of your hand(s). Keep your fingers in together.

The **Open Tones** are played on the edge of the drum that is closest to your body. When you're tapping the edge of the drum, you will let your hands rebound but you're only tapping the drum with your fingers and the top part of your palm(s). Please maintain the triangle shape with your fingers together and that will keep your thumbs off the drum head.

The **Slap Tones** are played in the same position as the open tones. For this tone the fingers are spread apart; still maintain the triangle shape to keep your thumbs off the drum head. Slap the drum and let your hands rebound.

The **Heel/Toe Tones** are performed by rocking your hand(s) beginning with your palm and ending with your fingers.

Heel = palm of hand ➡

Toe = fingers of hand ➡

Let your hands rock

POSTURE / HELPFUL HINTS

Proper posture is essential when playing various types of hand drums and percussion instruments.

When you are sitting and playing your hand drum it is important that you sit at the edge of your chair. Maintain your posture by keeping your back straight and your **arms, shoulders and wrists relaxed**.

It is very important to keep the drum **slanted away from your body**. This will provide you with a **larger playing surface** and it will allow the **sound to escape** from the bottom of the drum.

Spend some time stretching to loosen your muscles before you play your drums. Do not forget to take deep breaths before and during your drum practices/drum circle sessions.

WARM – UP STUDIES
INTRODUCTION TO BOX NOTATION

Focus on staying relaxed and let your hands rebound off your hand drum.

Hand Drumming Exercises: R = Right Hand, L = Left Hand

B = Bass Tone
O = Open Tone
S = Slap Tone

1)
| B | B | B | B | O | O | O | O | B | B | B | B | O | O | O | O |

R L R L
L R L R etc.

2)
| B | B | O | O | B | B | O | O | B | B | O | O | B | B | O | O |

R L R L
L R L R etc.

3)
| B | B | O | O | B | B | S | S | B | B | O | O | B | B | S | S |

R L R L
L R L R etc.

4)
| O | O | B | B | O | O | S | S | O | O | B | B | O | O | S | S |

R L R L
L R L R etc.

CREATE YOUR OWN BOX NOTATION

If a box is blank, leave it as a rest.

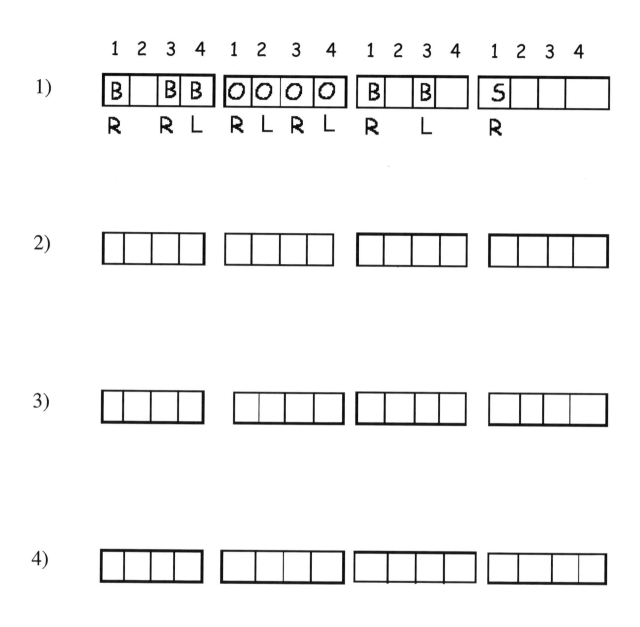

Have fun creating your own rhythms.

CHAPTER 2

IMPORTANT MUSIC CONCEPTS

Music Concepts

Collins Gem. Dictionary of Music, 1980.

Beat: "unit of measurement in music"

Rhythm: "organization of music in respect to time"

EXAMPLES

Tempo: "pace of composition as determined by speed of beat to which it is performed"

Time Signature: "indication at start of piece of music of number and type of note values in each bar"

Example

4 = Top number tells you how many beats each bar receives
4 = Bottom number tells you the value of each beat

RHYTHM SOUNDS / TERMINOLOGY

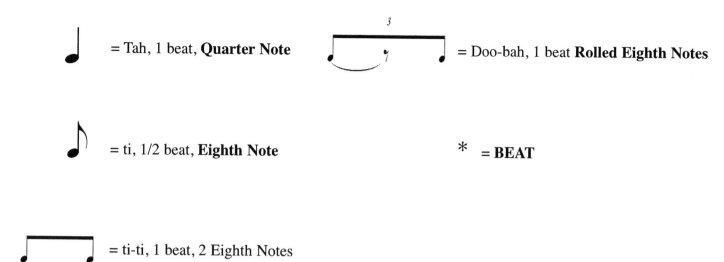

♩ = Tah, 1 beat, **Quarter Note**

= Doo-bah, 1 beat **Rolled Eighth Notes**

♪ = ti, 1/2 beat, **Eighth Note**

* = **BEAT**

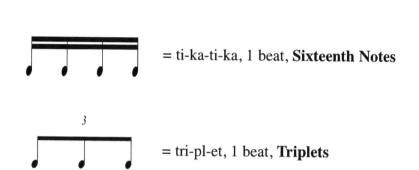

= ti-ti, 1 beat, 2 Eighth Notes

= ti-ka-ti-ka, 1 beat, **Sixteenth Notes**

= tri-pl-et, 1 beat, **Triplets**

SILENT REST SIGNS

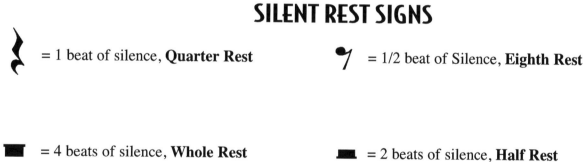

= 1 beat of silence, **Quarter Rest**

= 1/2 beat of Silence, **Eighth Rest**

= 4 beats of silence, **Whole Rest**

= 2 beats of silence, **Half Rest**

CHAPTER 3

RHYTHM STUDIES, READING MUSIC

INSTRUCTIONAL CONCEPTS

The following are some pointers that you can use to make your students comfortable with reading music and playing their drums or percussion instruments.

Follow the next four steps to have your students/participants develop their music reading skills. Have Fun!

Step #1: Have everyone sing only the rhythm.

Step #2: Demonstrate how to sing the rhythm and clap the beat

Step #3: Now have them play the rhythm studies on their hand drums. Play the rhythm studies as open tones. Explain to your students that it is important to alternate hands leading with their stronger hand.

Step # 4: The next important step is to encourage your students to tap their toe to the beat. It also helps if you keep the beat using a cowbell.

FURTHER SUGGESTIONS TO HELP YOUR STUDENTS MEET SUCCESS

Photocopy the rhythm studies to use on an overhead projector then have your students/participants sing the rhythm and clap the beat as a group. Point to the notes as your class follows along.

Encourage your students/participants to maintain eye contact with you at all times and to listen to each other to develop musicality. Developing music reading skills through eye contact with the director is a very important skill.

Demonstrate how to play a variety of percussion instruments then distribute the instruments and play through the rhythm studies as a group.

Divide up your drum circle and have each section perform one of the assigned rhythm studies.

Once your students/participants have played all the rhythm studies as open tones, have them go through and play all the **Tah Tones (Quarter Notes)** as **Bass Tones**.

Play through all of the rhythm studies using drum sticks. Maintain the fulcrum and encourage everyone to let the drum sticks rebound off the drum head. Focus on having everyone relaxed and maintain an upside down V shape above the drum.

Using a variety of drums and percussion instruments, divide up your drum circle and have each section perform one of the assigned rhythm studies. Let your Drum Circle know to be prepared to enter on cue and perform the ending rhythm on cue. Refer to the **Tah & ti-ti Rhythm Drum Circle Experience** on the DVD/Chapter 9.

THE TAH & TI-TI RHYTHMS

1)

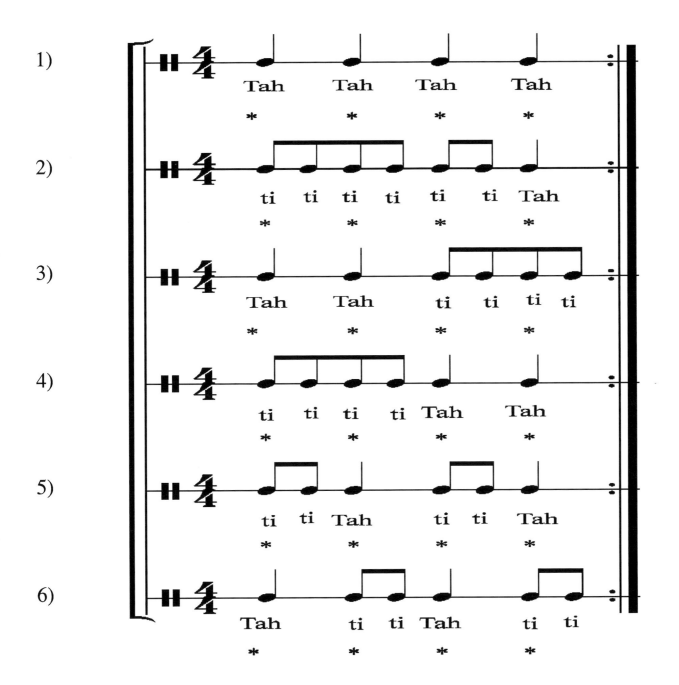

7)

The drum circle facilitator is to cue the ensemble to play this rhythm to end the Tah & ti-ti Drum Circle Experience.

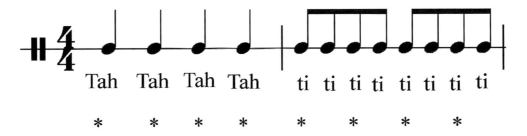

MORE RHYTHM STUDIES

1)

The drum circle facilitator is to cue the ensemble to play this rhythm to end this Syncopated Drum Circle Experience.

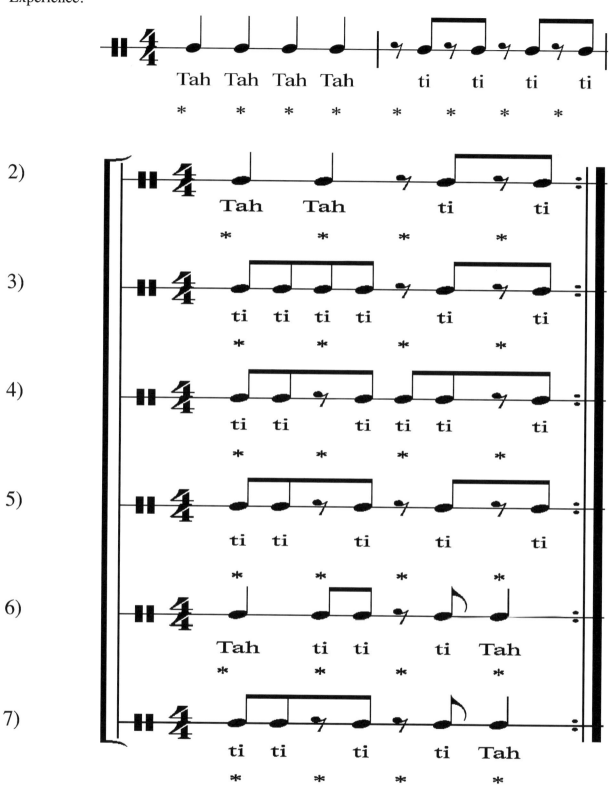

Practice slowly, sing and play the rhythm on your drum or percussion instrument. Tap your foot to the beat to help maintain the tempo. Have Fun!

THE TRI-PL-ET RHYTHMS

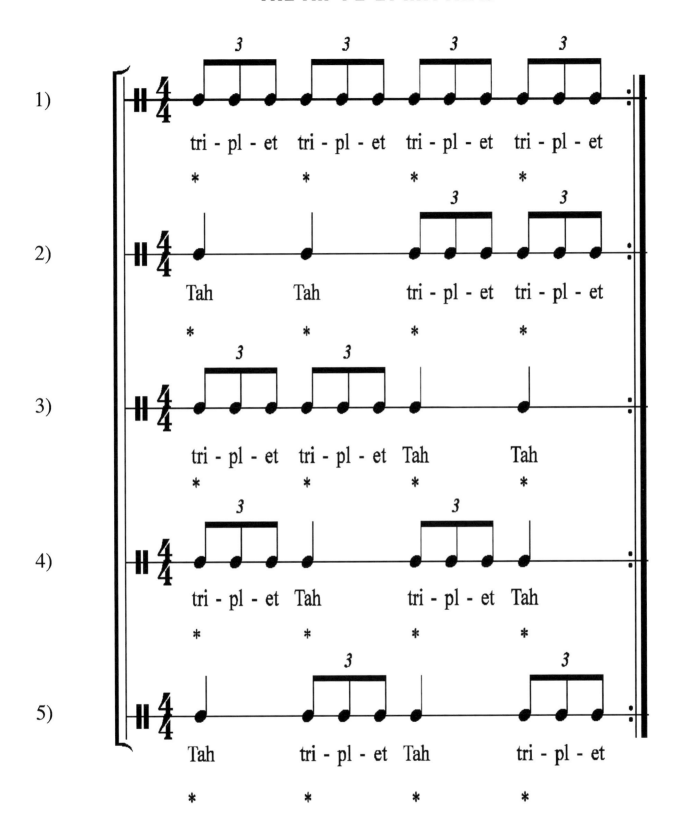

THE DOO-BAH RHYTHMS

Make sure that you let the first eighth note resonate longer than the second eighth note (SWING the EIGHTH NOTES).

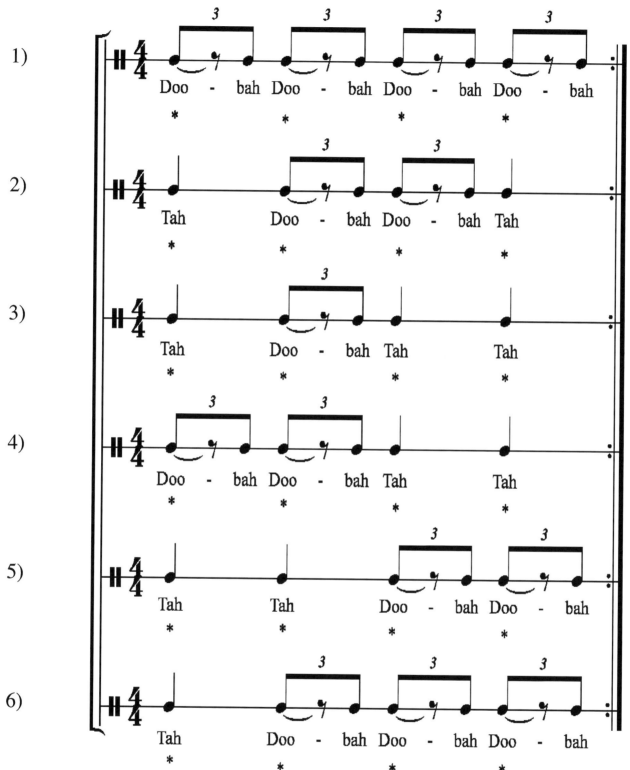

THE DOO-BAH & TRI-PL-ET RHYTHM COMBINATIONS

This is just a reminder that it is important to alternate hands starting with your stronger hand. Practice slowly at first and focus on staying relaxed. I suggest that you practice with a metronome or a drum machine. Get together with a friend(s) to practice and to communicate musically.

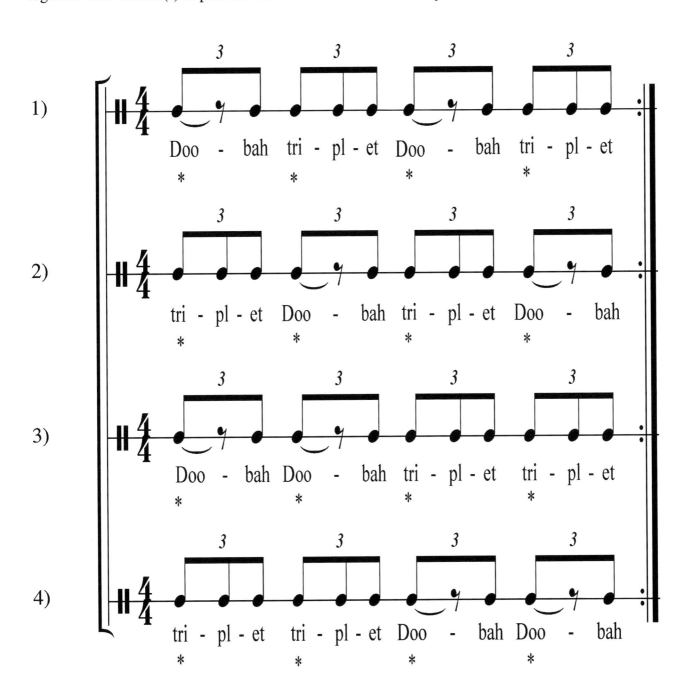

THE TI-KA-TI-KA RHYTHMS

1)

ti - ka - ti - ka ti - ka - ti - ka ti - ka - ti - ka ti - ka - ti - ka

*   *   *   *

2)

The drum circle facilitator is to cue the ensemble to play this rhythm to end the ti-ka-ti-ka Drum Circle Experience.

This is just a friendly reminder that it is important to lead with your stronger hand and alternate hand patterns.

CHAPTER 4

MORE HAND DRUMMING TECHNIQUES

IMPORTANT REMINDERS FOR HAND DRUMMING

Fingers, arms, hands must remain relaxed.

Hands straight forward in line with arms, don't curve your wrists inwards.

Mainly use wrists and forearm motion when playing your hand drum.

Maintain proper posture.

Keep the drum slanted away from your body so that the sound can escape from below.

Focus on practicing slow and concentrate on sound projection. Don't forget to create a triangle shape in the middle of your hands and let your hands/fingers rebound off the drum head.

 B = Bass Tones = Goon / Doon

O = Open Tones = Goe / Doe

S = Slap Tones = Pah / Tah

H/T = Heel/Toe Tones: Let your hand(s) rock between your palm and fingers (together).

* = Beat

Alternate hands starting with your dominant hand.

WARM-UP STUDIES FOR HAND DRUMMING

Getting Comfortable with Sound Projection and Hand Drumming Techniques

1)

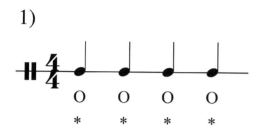

2)

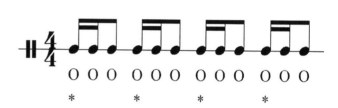

3)

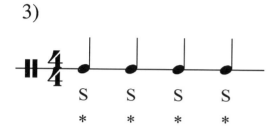

4)

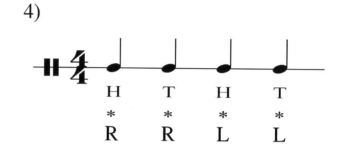

5)

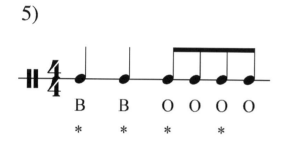

6)

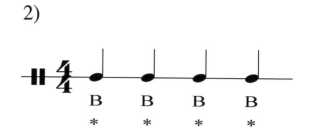

7)

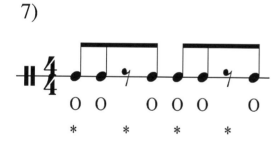

8)

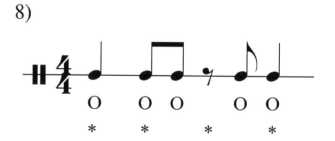

9)

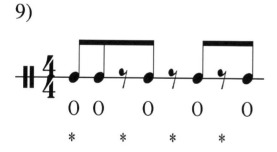

Start at a slow tempo and gradually speed up the tempo. Just before you tense up, slow the tempo back down so that all of your muscles are relaxed. Alternate between hands leading with your dominant hand.

Be aware of the Heel Toe Tones when playing/practicing these exercises. Make sure that your hand(s) do a rocking motion between your palms and fingers. Fingers must stay in together (H = Palm, T = Fingers).

10)

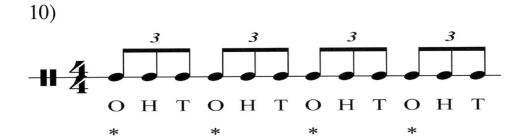

11)

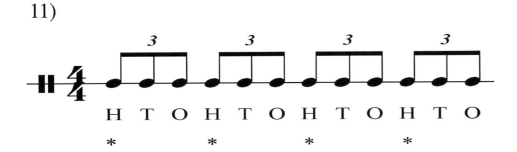

12)

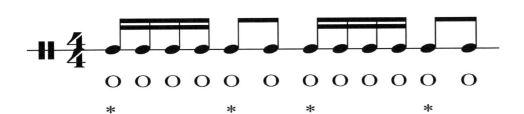

13)

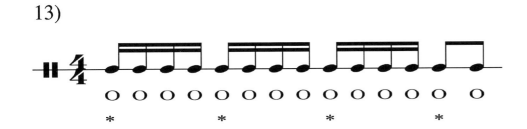

14)

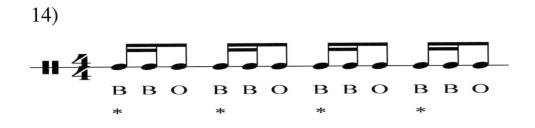

15)

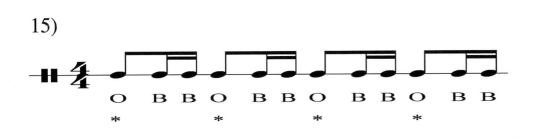

CHAPTER 5

THE FOUR ESSENTIAL RUDIMENTS

MAINTAIN YOUR FULCRUM
WHERE IS THE FULCRUM LOCATED?

This is a common question. It is very important that you maintain a comfortable grip with your sticks/and or mallets when you are playing drums. Here are some guidelines that you can follow to maintain a comfortable/ relaxed grip.

The **FULCRUM** is located between your **THUMB & INDEX FINGER**. Please make sure that your thumb rests flat on the side of the stick or mallet. The stick or mallet should be resting in the first groove of your index finger, make sure that your index finger is not above the thumb. Have the rest of your fingers gently touching the drum stick. Keep your hand(s), wrists, arms and shoulders relaxed when playing your **DRUM** or **PERCUSSION** instrument.

Make sure that the drum stick and/or the mallet bounces off the drum head or percussion instrument. Do not push the drum stick into the drum. If you are playing a snare drum, tenor drum or a drum where you need to use two sticks or mallets, maintain a triangle shape above the drum so that your palms are facing the ground. Let the sticks or mallets rebound off the drum head.

Thanks to Roger Flock, Don Vickery, and Paul DeLong who were my Percussion Professors at Humber College, Toronto and Jack Broumpton at Laurentian University in Sudbury.

Roger Flock and Don Vickery were my professors who opened my eyes to the World of Drumming and music education at my Humber College days back in the 1980's. It was these professors that began my love of music education.

THE FOUR ESSENTIAL RUDIMENTS

It is very important to take the time to practice and master these four important rudiments. I suggest that you spend some time at the beginning of your drum set/percussion practice by warming up through playing these four drum rudiments. Always start slowly, build up the tempo and always slow back down. It is important to maintain your grip and stay relaxed (maintain your FULCRUM). Always let your sticks rebound off the drum and begin to slow the tempo (SPEED) down before you begin to tighten up.

1) Singles

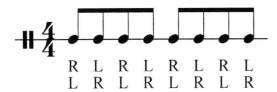

```
R L R L R L R L
L R L R L R L R
```

2) Doubles

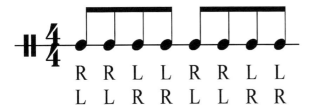

```
R R L L R R L L
L L R R L L R R
```

3) Single Paradiddle

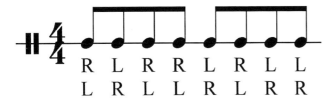

```
R L R R L R L L
L R L L R L R R
```

4) Multiple Bounce Roll

```
R L R L R L R L R L R L R L R L
L R L R L R L R L R L R L R L R
```

Let your drum stick fall and bounce when practicing the multiple bounce roll. Do not slide your drum sticks across the drum head. Maintain a straight up and down motion.

PAUL DELONG

Paul DeLong is a fantastic drummer and educator. Over the three years that I studied with Paul, he encouraged me to follow my heart with regards to pursuing my interest in music education. Paul opened a lot of musical doors for me to become a more rounded musician through his encouragement.

Thanks Paul!

CHAPTER 6
HAVE FUN PLAYING AUXILIARY PERCUSSION INSTRUMENTS

AUXILIARY PERCUSSION

Today's popular music incorporates many percussion instruments reflecting the diversity of cultures in our communities. Take the time to learn to play a variety of auxiliary percussion instruments.

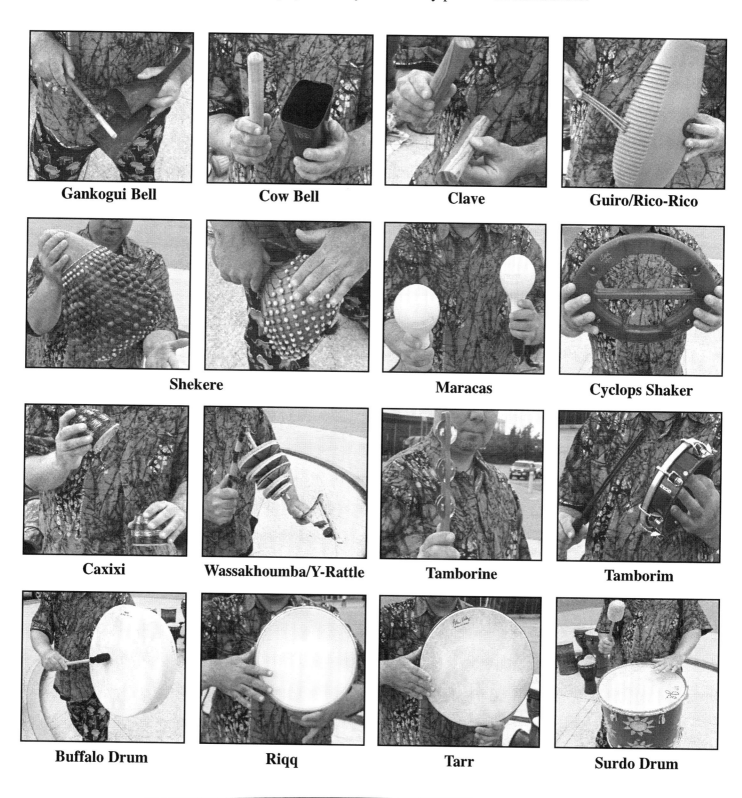

Gankogui Bell   **Cow Bell**   **Clave**   **Guiro/Rico-Rico**

Shekere   **Maracas**   **Cyclops Shaker**

Caxixi   **Wassakhoumba/Y-Rattle**   **Tamborine**   **Tamborim**

Buffalo Drum   **Riqq**   **Tarr**   **Surdo Drum**

HAVE FUN PLAYING AUXILIARY PERCUSSION INSTRUMENTS USING THE RHYTHM STUDY PAGES

Teachers and/or Drum Facilitators can have their students participate playing a variety of shakers, cowbells, wood blocks, two tone bells or frame drums, tambourines and tamborims. These instruments will add layers of textural sounds to your drum circles.

Divide up your class or group into sections (3-6 groups) and assign specific rhythm studies to each group. Demonstrate how to hold and to play each percussion instrument as you hand them out to the students. Allow each group to play their rhythm for a few bars before counting in the next group.

If you don't have shakers or drums, you can create your own drums and percussion instruments like my friend **Steve Sheehan**. Have your students make their own drums and shakers out of items such as large water bottles (call your local water company for donations of old water containers), coffee cans, and plastic containers. Old mini film strip containers can be made into egg shakers, tall chip containers can be shakers and if you add a wooden dowel for a drumstick you can create a drum. You can have your students decorate their instruments with multi- coloured duct tape, paper mache, paint, or beads. Add beans, popcorn, seeds, rice, spaghetti or experiment with different combinations for shaker sounds. Remember to ask students to donate some of the items you need to create your own percussion instruments.

CHAPTER 7

THREE PART RHYTHM DRUM CIRCLE FUN!

Divide and assign each group a rhythm. Signal and count each group in one at a time. Give each group a few measures (4 bars) before signalling in the next group. Review the rhythms with the entire group then divide up your drum circle into three groups. There is also a multiple percussion part available to be used along with the "Three Part Rhythm Drum Circle Fun" Extravaganza.

LETS GROOVE, TAH & TI-TI RHYTHMS

Have your drum circle sing each rhythm part before you play the parts on the drums/percussion instruments **(Tah & ti-ti etc.).**

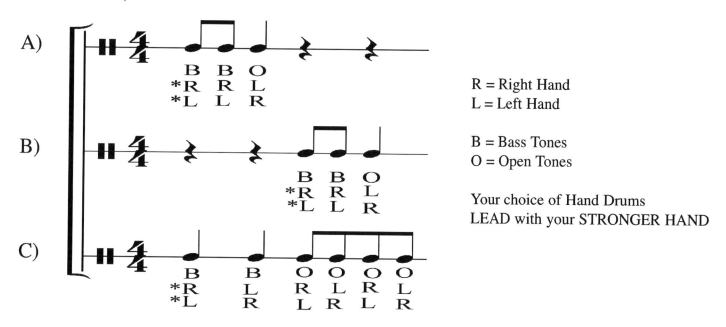

R = Right Hand
L = Left Hand

B = Bass Tones
O = Open Tones

Your choice of Hand Drums
LEAD with your STRONGER HAND

AUXILIARY PERCUSSION PARTS

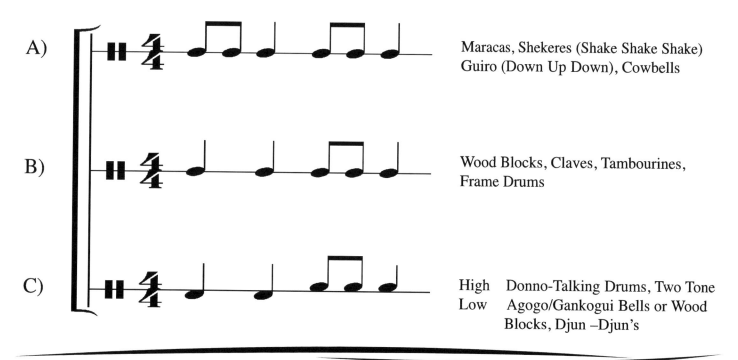

A) Maracas, Shekeres (Shake Shake Shake)
Guiro (Down Up Down), Cowbells

B) Wood Blocks, Claves, Tambourines, Frame Drums

C) High   Donno-Talking Drums, Two Tone
Low   Agogo/Gankogui Bells or Wood
Blocks, Djun –Djun's

WE ALL RAP AND PLAY SOME DRUMS

I wrote a short song for one of the school's where I teach here in Sudbury (Alexander P.S.). The original title is called "Alligator Rap" that is featured in the DVD. Our school logo is "Alligators" so I thought it would be fun to use this short drum rap as a way to build my students' and school morale when we have presentations in the gymnasium.

Please feel free to change the **"We all Rap"** to suit your school logo or community environment. Begin by having your drum circle RAP and then have them move into playing the **"Three Part, Lets GROOVE (Tah - ti-ti)"**.

GET READY TO RAP!

Sing Your RAP! ------------- then----------- Play On Your DRUM!
We all Rap,	*Goon Goon, Doe*
We all Drum,	*Goon Goon, Doe*
Let's Play Our Drums,	*Goon Goon, Doe*

Show our Spirit by playing right NOW!

Have your drum circle go into playing the **"Lets GROOVE (Tah - ti-ti)" Drum Circle Experience** and signal your students or participants to go back into the rap.

Echo/Call and Response: The lead drummer will signal everyone to stop playing. Make sure that you stress the importance of eye contact so that the participants can be guided through the highly spirited drum circle experience. After the lead drummer has signalled to stop, the lead drummer or a drum circle participant will **play** a rhythm on their drum or percussion instrument and the rest of the participants will **answer** back with the same rhythm. The lead drummer will then signal everyone to come back in with their part. This will add a lot of **SPIRIT** in your drum circle. The Echo/Call and Response can also be used with other drum circle experiences. I want to thank Doug Sole for sharing his knowledge of facilitating drum circles.

TRI-PL-ET & DOO-BAH GROOVE TIME

Make sure that when your group sings/plays the Doo-bah rhythms that they sing the first eighth note and let the drum tone resonate a little longer than the second eighth note.

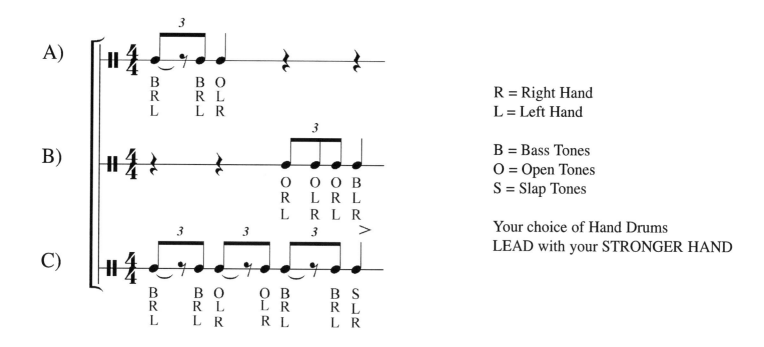

R = Right Hand
L = Left Hand

B = Bass Tones
O = Open Tones
S = Slap Tones

Your choice of Hand Drums
LEAD with your STRONGER HAND

AUXILIARY PERCUSSION PARTS

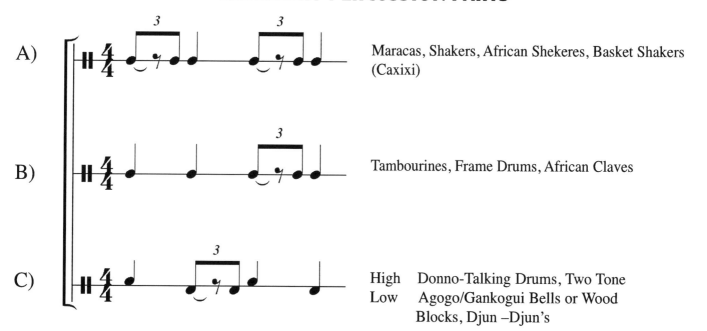

Maracas, Shakers, African Shekeres, Basket Shakers (Caxixi)

Tambourines, Frame Drums, African Claves

High   Donno-Talking Drums, Two Tone
Low   Agogo/Gankogui Bells or Wood
        Blocks, Djun –Djun's

THE DJEMBE AFRICAN NANINGO GROOVE

You or one of your drum circle participants can play the African Naningo Cultural Specific Djembe part over the Three Part Triplet and Doo-bah Groove. By layering these triplet grooves over top the result will be a 6/8 African Naningo Feel.

In the video presentation, I called upon a part of my talented drum circle to echo me on a call & response. Using this echoing is a technique found in many African forms of music.

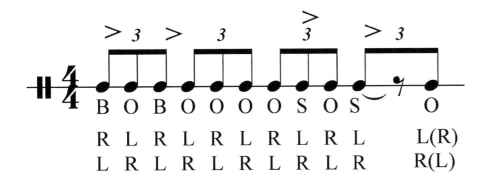

Play the bracket (R) (L) hand position before going to the below Variation using the Heel Toe Tone.

Play the above African Naningo Djembe Groove for the length of seven bars. Then play the bottom variation on the eighth bar and go back to the above cultural specific Djembe groove.

Variation using the Heel Toe Tone

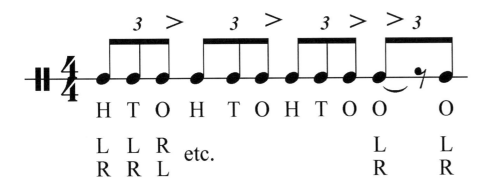

THE TI-KA-TI-KA & TI-TI RHYTHM GROOVE TIME

Make sure that when your drum circle participants are singing and playing these rhythms that they don't rush. There is always a tendency to want to rush the tempo when playing sixteenth note patterns. Tell them to just relax and sit into the tempo and the GROOVE.

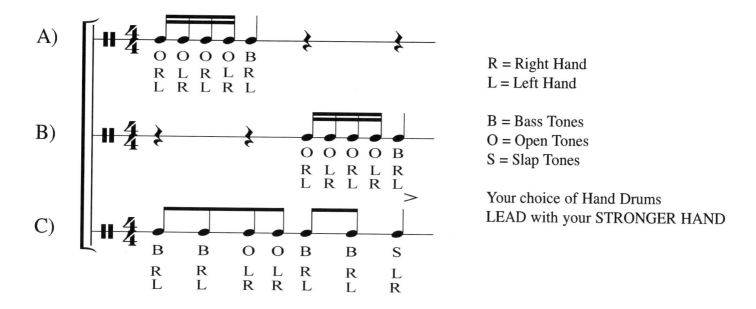

R = Right Hand
L = Left Hand

B = Bass Tones
O = Open Tones
S = Slap Tones

Your choice of Hand Drums
LEAD with your STRONGER HAND

AUXILIARY PERCUSSION PARTS

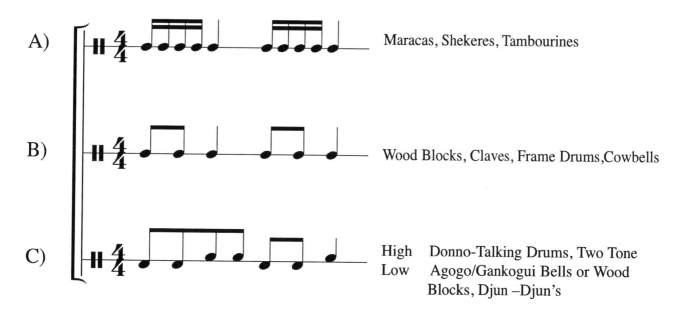

A) Maracas, Shekeres, Tambourines

B) Wood Blocks, Claves, Frame Drums, Cowbells

C) High   Donno-Talking Drums, Two Tone
Low   Agogo/Gankogui Bells or Wood
Blocks, Djun –Djun's

HAVE FUN USING BOOMWHACKERS
"FUN AND JOY"

I have composed a four part Boomwhacker composition that can be performed with the **ti-ka-ti-ka and ti-ti Three Part Drum Circle Experience**. Combining Boomwhackers with drumming is a **BLAST** of **"FUN and JOY"** and it creates a melodic drum circle environment.

Cue each Boomwhacker part one at a time. Give each section a few bars (4 Bars) before cueing in the next parts. Once you have the Boomwhacker **"Fun and Joy"** HAPPENING then you can call upon your **drummers** to join in this great melodic drum circle **"FUN AND JOY"**.

"FUN AND JOY"

The following is the **Boomwhacker** four part composition that can be performed along with the **ti-ka-ti-ka and ti-ti Three Part Drum Circle Experience**. This drum circle experience combines a melodic approach with the combination of the C Diatonic Major set of Boomwhackers.

Divide up your Boomwhacker participants into four groups. Assign each group a part. Organize your drummers into a large semi-circle. The part # 1 Boomwhacker section needs to be standing up in front of the drummers. Have the boomwhacker parts # 2, 3 and 4 sitting inside the circle. Organize the participants in a way that you can easily move around and in between the **"Fun and Joy"** Ensemble to facilitate.

Part # 1 will be using a drum stick and their thigh to perform their part. The rest of the ensemble will be performing their parts on the floor through the use of two assigned Boomwhackers per participant. Remind them to let the Boomwhackers rebound off the floor. Hold the Boomwhackers the same proper way you hold a pair of drum sticks. Maintain the **FULCRUM**.

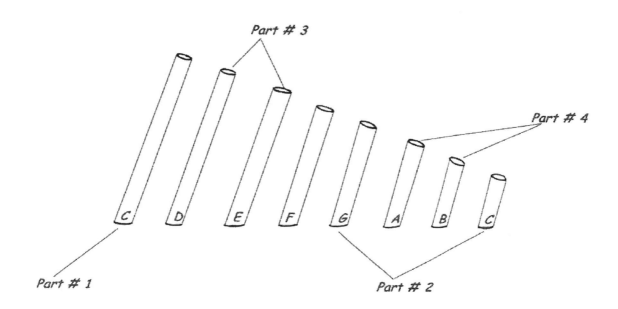

"FUN AND JOY"

Part # 1: The participants who play this part will need to use a drum stick along with the Large C Boomwhacker. The Goon Tone (G) is to be played by tapping your thigh and for the Pah (P) tone tap the end of the Boomwhacker with a drum stick
(Thanks to Doug Sole, my MENTOR).

Part # 1 participants will need to stand up in front of your drum circle participants to comfortably perform their part.

Part # 1 _Low C_= weaker hand * G = Thigh Tone / P = Stick Tone

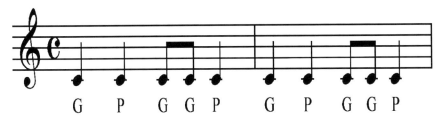

Begin by cueing in each part one at a time. Starting with part # 1 and continue to cue the other parts after every four bars; then have the drum circle enter.

Part # 2: G/_High C_ = stronger hand

Part # 3: E/_D_ = stronger hand

Part # 2, 3, and 4 are to be performed by having the participants sitting on the floor so that they can perform the parts by striking their assigned Boomwhackers on the floor. Let the Boomwhackers rebound off the floor.

Part # 4: A/_B_ = stronger hand * U = "Tap together up in the air", Bing Bang Boomwhackers, Volume # 1.

CHAPTER 8

EXPERIENCE THE SPIRIT OF WORLD MUSIC

LIVE LIFE TO THE FULLEST

Drumming plays an important part in the life and culture of the great contribution Native music has made to the world.

As stated by Will Morin. The **heart ode (o-day)** plays an important role with the **drum dewegan (day-way-gun)**. Drumming will bring people together into a positive spiritual light and dimension.

Will Morin has also written a poem that will be performed with the community drum circle experience that will help bring people together into a positive spiritual light, **"Can You Hear It?"**.

Will Morin is Spiritually like a brother to me.

NATIVE GATHERING DRUM CIRCLE EXPERIENCE

Begin by facilitating a sound sculpture of rain sounds with the hand drums using finger tips in a circular motion. Have some of the participants use rain sticks, ocean and thunder drums. End the sound sculpture then signal the Gathering Drum, which is the heartbeat (ode), to begin. Lead each of the frame drum parts in one at a time. Finish the Drum Circle the same way you began with the sound sculpture.

A) Buffalo Drum (Large Frame Drum)

Edge = *Near the rim of Frame Drum*
Middle = *Middle of Frame Drum*

Edge
Middle

B) Medium Frame Drum

Edge
Middle

C) Medium Frame Drum

Edge
Middle

D) Small Frame Drum

Edge
Middle

Community Gathering Drum Part (2-4 Participants on one DRUM)

Can you hear it

Can you hear it, Can you hear it?
Can you? Can you? Can you hear it?

Falling, Floating, Flying
I can feel the sounds drums make
I can feel the sounds chimes make.
I feel the wind, its force, its song.
I feel its texture soothing soft.
I touch its meaning when it engulfs me.
Exposed flesh transmits to the rest.

Floating on star dust, nothing in my way, shhhh, Listen!
The Raven is calling, cawing, floating on feathers that cut the air.
This muse is my Bird of Pray, fanning for words to say.
Choosing words more than meaning, flapping, cawing, calling
A message I hear floating.
floating, floating, floating, floating, floating, floating, floating

Wing tips spread, fingers wide, guide me to where clouds house
a child's world beyond reality, Where all is possible and is.
To open minds, imaginations alive. So soft and pure,
I reach to touch and tingle as feathers fan out,
and the air caresses me.
The message I feel, I'm floating, floating, floating, floating.

Floating on spring rain drops, nothing in my way, shhhh, Listen.
Can you hear the water of your birth?
Can you hear the cries of Mother Earth?
Can you hear her drum beat of worth?
Can you hear the cries of Mother Earth?

Can you hear it, Can you feel it, the heartbeat of the drum?
Sing it, taste it, drink it, live it when you hummmm, when you hummm.

Can you hear it, Can you hear it?
Can you? Can you? Can you hear it?

My spirit is a single feather that was plucked from the Eagle
that has fallen centuries ago.
Speaking in silent motion I hope to reach the hearts and the drums
of those who seek connection.

Earth Dancers Performance 2005, Music by: *Sudbury World Drum Circle*.
© 2005 William Morin

THE CUBAN CLAVE

What is the importance of the Clave Rhythm?

The Clave Rhythm is the **"Key Code"** or the **"Keystone"** of how Latin American music is composed and arranged. The Clave **"governs the flow of the music"** (Latin Sounds From The Drum Set).

There are two different types of the two-bar Clave Rhythm.

Forward Clave:

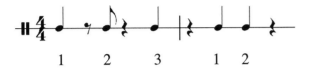

Reverse Clave:

Even though they are the same rhythm it is very important to be *aware* of the *Forward* and the *Reverse Clave Rhythm*. All of the percussion, music and melodic parts are composed around the clave rhythm.

The Clave Rhythm also plays a very important role with regards to the phrasing. When listening and performing Latin American music, it is very important to be aware of the forward and reverse clave in conjunction with the melody. The arrangement may start in a forward clave form and then change to the reverse clave in the bridge section of the tune by subtracting or adding a bar to an equal bar phrase.

Example:

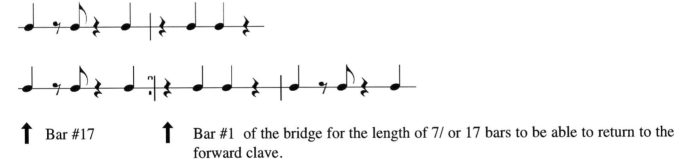

↑ Bar #17   ↑ Bar #1 of the bridge for the length of 7/ or 17 bars to be able to return to the forward clave.

CUBAN 2/3 CLAVE, CHA! CHA! CHA!

"Cha - Chalaca is a Spanish - French twittering of a bird"
(Latin Sounds From The Drum Set)

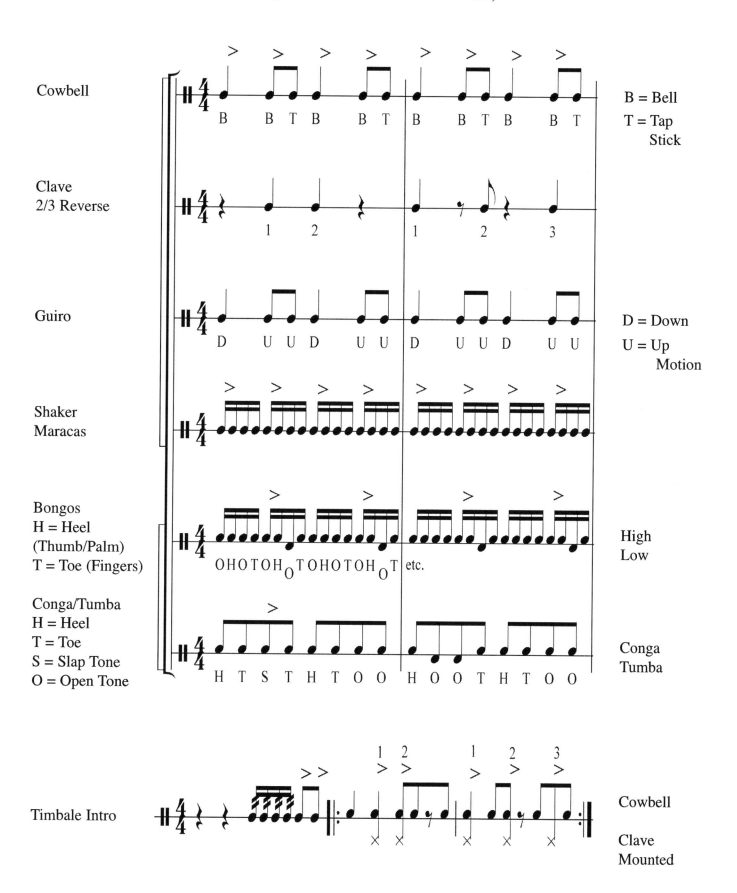

DREAM PULSE

Dream Pulse is an introduction to Japanese Kodo Drumming

Please review the proper way to hold drum sticks/mallets. Participants will need to use mallets and drum sticks to perform the "Dream Pulse" Japanese Kodo Drum CIRCLE Experience.

Have your students and/or your community drum circle participants play/practice through the Rhythm studies using drum sticks. Make sure that they stay relaxed and let the drum sticks bounce. Maintain the FULCRUM.

JAPANESE KODO DRUMMING EXPERIENCE

Kodo Drums or use a variety of Tom Toms/Concert Bass Drums or Timpani's.

Have each part come in one at a time. Start with the Gong, three Temple Block part and then add in each Taiko (huge barrel Kodo Drum) part, one at a time. Then add in each part one at a time starting with the Xylophone/Marimba/Flute and/or a keyboard that can create the Xylophone, Marimba or Shakuhachi (bamboo flute) sounds.

To end Dream Pulse, you the drum facilitator will need to cue the ensemble to perform the ending section in unison.

Spend some time with your students or participants listening to a variety of music that use the pentatonic scale. Have them practice creating music using the five note pentatonic scale.

**Thanks to Carolyn Otto & to her talented
Sudbury Secondary Students
of the Fine Music Arts Program
for their Outstanding Performance**

DREAM PULSE, KODO JAPANESE EXPERIENCE

Taiko (Kodo) Drum/Percussion Instruments

Gong: (Gong mallet) Whole Note receives 4 beats, two Whole Notes that are tied together will receive 8 beats of sound: So let the Gong ring for 8 beats.
Temple Blocks: Three Temple Blocks or Wood Blocks, (Two mallets)

1) **Kodo Drum/Bass Drum or Timpani**: If you decide to use a Timpani please tune it to F which is the Tonic note of the F pentatonic key.
(Two Soft Mallets)

2) **Kodo Drum/Floor Tom or Bass drum**:
(Two Soft mallets)

3) **Kodo Drums or Two Tom Toms**: Two yarn mallets or drum sticks with taped felt wrapped around the ends of the drum sticks.

Ostinato Ending on cue by the Drum facilitator

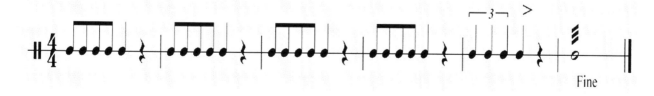

Fine

Create a thundering **Kodo Drum Sound** to end kof this **"Dream Pulse"** musical experience.

DREAM PULSE, KODO JAPANESE EXPERIENCE

Xylophone/Marimba/Flute Five Note F Pentatonic Melody Parts

Xylophone/Marimba/Flute: These parts are an Ostinato melody which is repeated until the cue to play the ending. Have your participants maintain eye contact so that they can enter on the cues. Have Fun!

Xylophone

Marimba

Flute

Ending to be played on cue:

A MIDDLE EASTERN MUSICAL EXPERIENCE

The next cultural specific drum experience will focus on using a variety of drums that are commonly used in the middle eastern countries for ceremonial traditional forms of music and dance. I have also noticed a variety of these percussion instruments used in today's electro -pop forms of music.

Doumbek: Holding the Doumbek is very different from holding a Djembe. It is very important to get yourself into the proper sitting position. Please sit towards the front of your chair with back straight and muscles must always be in a relaxed state. Take your goblet shaped Doumbek and rest the body of it onto the thigh of your raised leg. Feel free to put a very small riser under that foot. Have the drum head facing in a forward position. Rest your weaker arm on top of the Doumbek's body with your fingers hanging over the top with the thumb resting on the rim.

Your stronger hand will perform the various tones from the other side of your Doumbek. Your hands will be in an inverted L shape form over top of your Doumbek's drum head (see DVD/Diagram). I strongly suggest using a long belt or a long luggage strap around your waist and the Doumbek to help keep the drum in place. This will also free your weaker hand to perform a larger variety of Doumbek Tones. Thanks Emilio for this idea! There are several unique tones that can be created on the Doumbek.

D = Doum (Bass Tone)
Stronger hand will tap the middle of the Doumbek using a combination of your three middle fingers. It is very important to let your fingers rebound off the head quickly.

t = tek (Open Natural Tone)
T = Tek (High Pitched Accented Open Tone)
Stronger hand will tap towards the rim using your middle finger to create open tones.

K = Kah (Weaker Hand Tek Tones)
Tap towards the rim using your middle or your ring finger to create open tones.

Sn = (Snap your fingers) using your weaker hand so that the "middle finger strikes" close to the rim of the drum head to produce a high pitched Tek tone (Doumbec delight).

FR = (Finger roll) by using the four fingers of your stronger/weaker hand in a Doum/Kah position. Start with your pinkie finger and finish the roll with your index finger creating a flick tone.

THE RIQQ AND TAR

The **Riqq** and **Tar** are percussion instruments from the frame drum family. Frame drums come in a variety of sizes and are used in a wide range of cultural forms of music.

The **Riqq** and the **Tar** are held in a similar position. Begin by holding the frame type drum with your weaker hand supporting the bottom part of the drum with your thumb resting on the inside part of the rim. Make sure that you have your thumb resting close to the jingles of the Riqq and have your middle finger actually resting on a set of jingles on the opposite side of the rim.

The thumb of the stronger hand can rest on the upper part of the rim/shell of both the **Riqq** and **Tar**. I suggest that you focus on **balancing** the **Riqq/Tar** with your weaker hand without your thumb having to always stay on the upper outside of the frame. This will allow you to have the fingers of your Dominant hand to move more freely to play the **Dun/Tak/tik Tones**.

The **Riqq** is a frame drum that has large jingles in comparison to a tambourine.

Upper Hand Tones

D = Dun (Bass Tone, Stronger Hand)
It is very important to tap the Riqq using the entire flat part of your **index finger** off centre from the middle of the Riqq's drum head. I also suggest that you angle the top part of the Riqq away from your body to help with regards to producing better tones.

T = Tak (Slap Tone, Stronger Hand)
Performed by tapping the very edge of the Riqq with your **middle finger** to produce a high pitch slap tone.

Lower Hand Tone

t = tik (Weaker Hand)
Jingle tone performed using the bottom hand. Place your thumb underneath the Riqq close to a set of jingles and then rest your middle finger on the jingle on the opposite side of your thumb. It is very important to play the tik tone in a **clear/quick technique**.

The **Tar** is a frame drum that is found in a variety of sizes.

Upper Hand Tone

D = Dun (Bass Tone)
Performed by tapping the drum head off centre using the flat part of your **index finger** to create a bass tone.

Alternating Hands

T = Tak (Stronger Hand), k = Ka (Weaker Hand)
Tap the Tar at the bearing edge of the drum using the middle fingers, alternating between both hands to create open tones.

To create proper Dun/Tak/Ka tones, it is very important to let your fingers rebound off the drum head to create resonant tones.

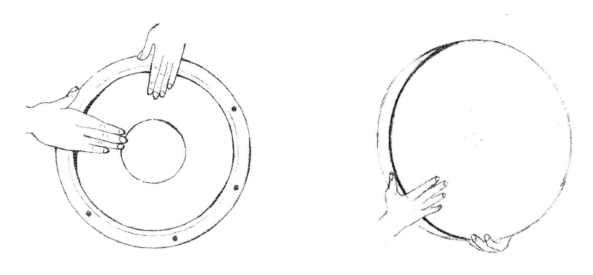

Doumbek Hand Position   **Tar Hand Position**

Riqq Hand Position:
Make sure that you
have your middle
finger of your weaker
hand resting on the
jingle.

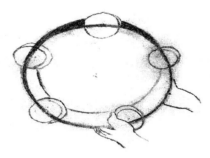

MIDDLE EASTERN FORMS OF DRUMMING

Please feel free to look to the side of the page to review the specific tone symbols.

Doumbek Grooves

A)

D k k D k k T k D k k D k k T k

B)

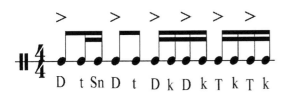

D t Sn D t D k D k T k T k

C)

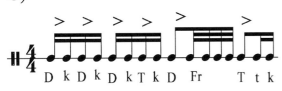

D k D k D k T k D Fr T t k

Riqq

D T t t T t t T t t T

Tar

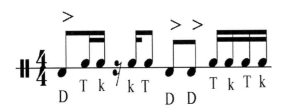

D T k k T D D T k T k

Doumbek Tones

Stronger Hand
D = Doum (Bass Tone)
T = Tek Tone (Open Accented Tone)
t = tek Tone (Open Natural Tone)

Other Hand
Ka = (Open Tones), sounds like tek
Open Tones
Sn = Snap thumb & Middle Finger
against drum head
Fr = Finger Roll (Pinkie to Index Finger)

Riqq Tones
D = Upper Hand, Dun Tone (Index Finger, Towards **Middle**)
T = Upper Hand, Tak Tone (Middle Finger, Towards **Edge**)
t - Lower Hand, tik Tone (**Jingle Tone**, Middle Finger)

Tar Tones
D = Dun (Index **Finger**, Bass Tone, Towards Middle) =
Dominant Hand
T/k = Tak/Ka (Middle **Fingers** of both hands, Open Tones,
Towards Edge) = **Alternating Hands**

EMILIO DOUMBEK DELIGHT

Emilio is a talented/educated percussionist. He has been sharing his knowledge of playing the African Djembe and the Doumbek with the community. The following is an arrangement by Emilio of culturally specific rhythms that can be performed in a community drum environment, or to accompany the Egyptian form of dancing.

Culturally Specific Doumbek Grooves

Intro: **Masmoodi**

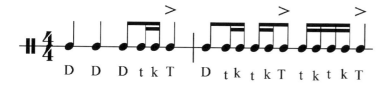

Saudi: A Doumbek pattern that can be performed over the Masmoodi.

Maksoum: Verses # 1 & 2   **Ayoob**: Choruses # 1 & 2

Sayidi: On the finale, feel free taking turns improvising between the Doumbek performers.

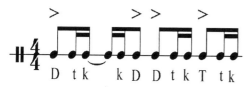

WINTER, SUMMER SAMBA

The Brazilian Samba is a very popular form of music. This form of music uses a wide variety of drums/percussion instruments which will get people up and dancing. Many of the percussion instruments and the Samba/Bossa Nova Styles are combined with Jazz & Pop forms of music.

Music Popular Brasileiro, habitually shorten to MPB, is the catch-all term Brazilians use for Brazilian music in general. It first cropped up in the 1930's.
WORLD MUSIC, THE ROUGH GUIDE: Published by Rough Guides Ltd. October 1994, 1 Mercer St. London, Reprinted 1995, Distributed by the Penguin Group. Some MPB Geography, pg. 558.

Thanks to Science North and to **Mark "Knowledge"** for your incredible job with your positive RAP!

THE SAMBA PERCUSSION INSTRUMENTS

The **Surdo Drum** plays an important role as the key drum that holds everything together like our heartbeat. It is important to use your weaker hand in conjunction with your stronger hand (that holds a mallet) to perform open and mute tones. You can use a floor tom to replace the Surdo Drum if you don't own one.

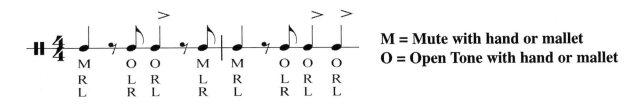

M = Mute with hand or mallet
O = Open Tone with hand or mallet

Agogo Bells are a two tone bell instrument that is originally from Africa (Gankogui Bell).

High
Low　Bell

Tamborims or make use of the **REMO Sound Shape Frame Drums** (Single Headed Drums).

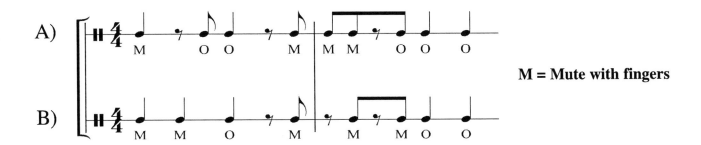

M = Mute with fingers

SAMBA BATACUDA (PERCUSSION) WINTER, SUMMER SAMBA

Conga/Tumba: All hand drums originate from Africa. Playing slap tones on the congas is different in comparison to playing the slap tones on the African Djembe. The type of slap tone you will be playing on the congas is a Latin American hand drumming technique. Begin by creating a **cup shape with your stronger hand**. When you go to perform a slap tone, it is like you're trying to grab hold of the drum head while slapping it to create an accented tone.

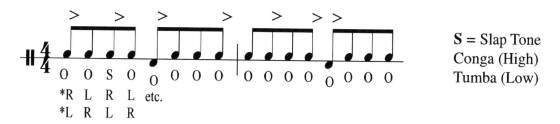

S = Slap Tone
Conga (High)
Tumba (Low)

Repinique: Is similar to a marching snare drum with the snares turned off. You can use two sticks or a combination of one stick and a hand to perform heel/toe tones. The lead drummer plays this instrument to signal and call upon cues in conjunction with a Three Tone Brazilian Whistle. Hold the **drum stick** with your **stronger hand** and **perform the Heel/Toe Tones with your weaker hand**.

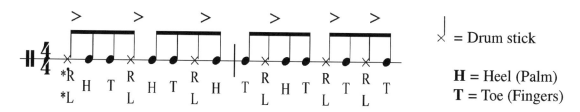

= Drum stick

H = Heel (Palm)
T = Toe (Fingers)

The **Caixa** is what we call the snare drum here in North America. It also plays an important role in the Brazilian Carnaval Samba.

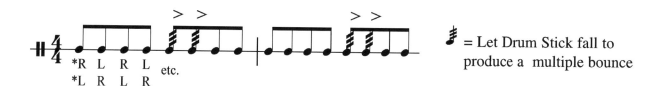

= Let Drum Stick fall to produce a multiple bounce

Pandeiro: A single headed tambourine: Even though this is a tambourine, there are many challenging rhythmic/technical parts to play in Brazilian music. Hold the Pandeiro with your **weaker hand** and **perform the tones** with your **stronger hand**.

F = Fingers
T = Thumb
O = Open Tones
(Towards the Edge of the Pandeiro)
M = Mute Tones
(Towards the Middle of the Pandeiro)

WINTER, SUMMER SAMBA

Samba Batacuda

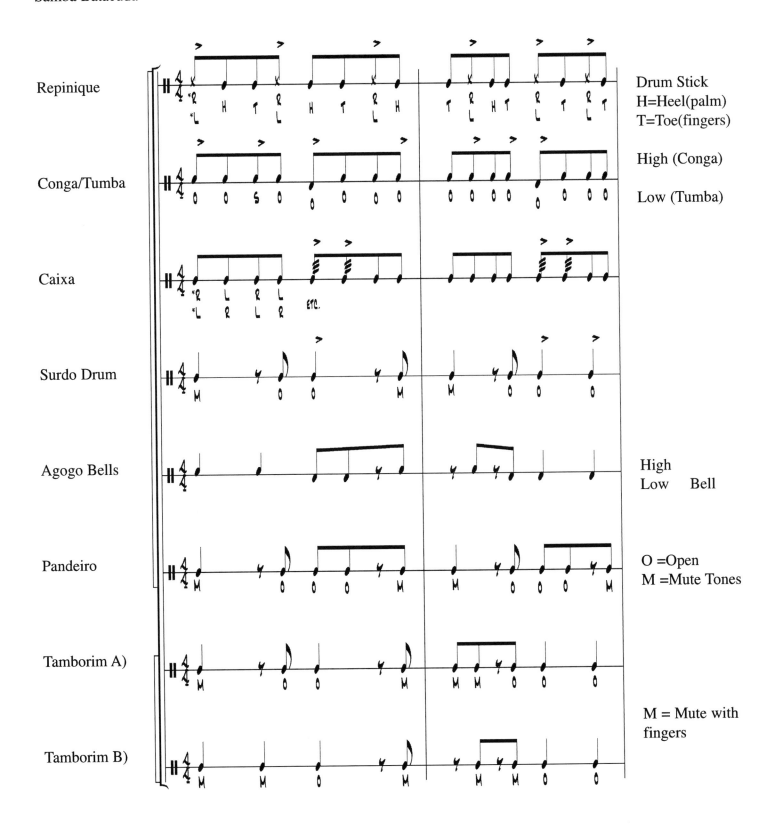

GHANA !!! HIGH LIFE
CULTURAL SPECIFIC AFRICAN DRUM EXPERIENCE

The lead drummer will always begin with playing an intro start rhythm to signal the rest of the drummers when to come in and to establish a tempo.

The intro start rhythm is also used to signal everyone in the drum circle to stop and to cue for Echo/Call and Response, so it is important to maintain eye contact and listen/respond to their playing/facilitation.

<u>Intro Start/Stop Rhythm</u>

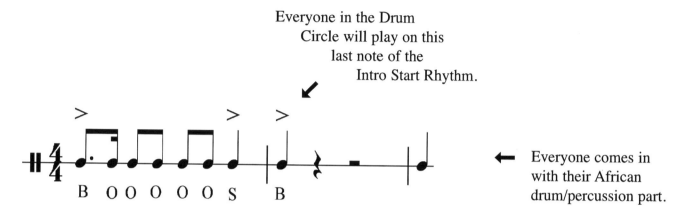

Everyone in the Drum
Circle will play on this
last note of the
Intro Start Rhythm.

B O O O O S   B

← Everyone comes in
with their African
drum/percussion part.

GHANA !!! HIGH LIFE

Are you ready to experience playing in a Ghana High Life Drum Circle?

Here is the breakdown of the specific hand drum and percussion parts.
A) Master Drum Part

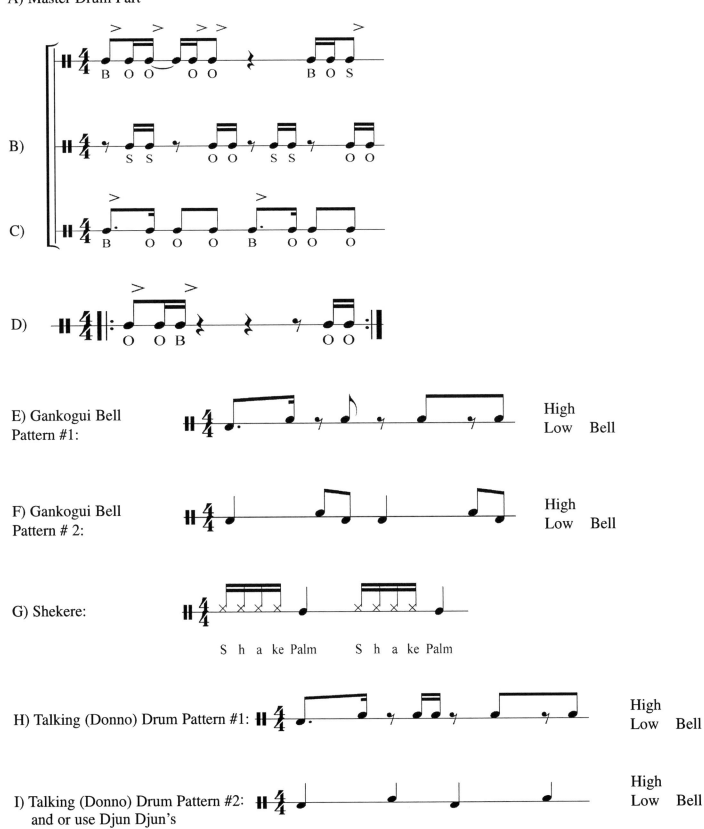

CHAPTER 9
EDUCATORS GUIDE TO SUCCESS
RUBRIC

Criteria	Level 1 (50-59%)	Level 2 (60-69%)	Level 3 (70-79%)	Level 4 (80-100%)
Performance * Demonstrates the proper playing techniques of drums/percussion instruments from around the WORLD	* demonstrates a **basic** level of the proper techniques	* demonstrates **some** of the proper techniques	* demonstrates **most** of the proper techniques	*Demonstrates a **high degree** of the proper techniques
Creating Music * Participates musically in a DRUM CIRCLE environment	* **rarely** participates	* **occasionally** participates	* **majority** of the time participates	* **fully** participates
Music Concepts * Beat, Rhythm, Textures, Dynamics, Tempo, Time Signatures How do they work together?	* demonstrates **little** understanding of how the music concepts work together	* demonstrates a **partial** understanding of how the music concepts work together	* demonstrates a **very good** understanding of how the music concepts work together	* demonstrates an **excellent** understanding of how the music concepts work together
Culture & Society * Communicates an understanding of the cultural styles/forms of music and where the instruments come from *(music response journals/group teamwork)*	* with **minimal** understanding	* with a **good** understanding	* with a **very good** understanding	* with an **excellent** understanding

THE SPIRIT OF WORLD DRUMMING, DRUM CIRCLE FUN FOR ALL AGES

EVALUATION ASSESSMENT

Using the criteria outlined below you can evaluate your students using either rubric levels, letter grades or a mark out of 10 for each skill (total of 50 marks).

Rubric Criteria
* Performance
Hand Drumming

Student Names	Sitting Position	Position of Hand Drum	Hand Position	Tone Production	Participation Musicality
Sheehan, Steve	4	4	3	3	4
Stewart, Jeff	4	4	3	4	4
Etc.					

* Performance
Percussion /Drums

Student Names	Posture	Position of Percussion Instrument	Hand(s)/ Stick -Mallet Position (fulcrum)	Tone Production	Participation Musicality
Sheehan, Steve	A-	B+	B+	B+	A+
Stewart, Jeff	B+	C+	B+	A-	A-
Etc.					

Rubric Criteria
*Creating Music

Student Names	Sense of Tempo	Beat in relation to Rhythm	Play Part Accurately	Proper Playing Technique	Expression Blending of Instrument Sound
Sheehan, Steve	3	3	3	3	4
Stewart, Jeff	4	4	3	3	3
Etc.					

* Creating Music

Student Names	Sense of Tempo	Rhythm Accuracy	Echo/Call & Response	Proper Sound Production	Expression Blending of Instrument Sound
Sheehan, Steve	8	8	7	7	8
Stewart, Jeff	7	7	8	7	8
Etc.					
Total Marks	10	10	10	10	10

Rubric Criteria
* Music Concepts

Student Names	Reading of Rhythm(s) (Kodaly System) Tah, ti-ti ti-ka-ti-ka Etc.	Clap/Tap beat while singing or playing the rhythm	Tempo/Time Signature	Sound Quality= Proper length of note values (Rhythm)	Expression
Sheehan, Steve	7	8	7	8	9
Stewart, Jeff	6	7	7	7	8
Etc.					
Total Marks	10	10	10	10	10

* Music Concepts

Student Names	Sense of Tempo	Dynamic Levels (Follows the Facilitator)	Rhythm Accuracy	Tone/Sound Production	Expression
Sheehan, Steve	4	3	3	3	3
Stewart, Jeff	4	4	3	3	3
Etc.					

Christine Stevens, Doug Sole
My Great Two Mentors
Orangeville Drum Circle Retreat

RUBRIC CRITERIA
*CULTURE AND SOCIETY

* Organize your class of talented students into 5 groups. Assign each group a question. Stress the importance of TEAM WORK. Young people must learn how to communicate their ideas to meet a common goal. Everyone in each one of the groups must have the opportunity to input their ideas to answer the question of cultural importance. Please record the name of the Artist(s)/Composer(s) or Band along with the name of the song on the blackboard. Play the recording several times so that all of the students can absorb the style, form and expression of the sound of music.

Group-Question # 1) Using the pictures of the auxiliary percussion instruments. Work together as a team to make a list of the drums/percussion instruments used in this recording.

Group-Question # 2) Teacher/Educator is to give this group the name of the country where this music originates from. Allow this group to use an atlas or better yet a large map. As a group they are to work together to locate the country of where the recorded music is from.

Group-Question # 3) Write a description of the recorded music.
- Tempo (How fast or Slow)
- Dynamics (Loud - Soft Volumes)
- State what you feel is the musical Style
- What instrument(s) or voice (male/female) is being used as the main feature?

Group-Question # 4) How does this song make us feel?
When was this song composed/recorded? (Estimate year, time of season)
Where do you think this style/form of music originates from?

Group-Question # 5) Why do you think the composer/band uses this title for the name of this song/recording?

Explain how the title represents the sound, feeling or meaning of this song?

* Allow time at the end of the class for the students to present there Group/Team findings. It's a choice if you would have all the students to respond to specific assigned questions. I also like to suggest the idea of each student having a music journal work book to respond to this question individually or even in a group/team setting.

SPECIFIC OBSERVATIONAL SKILLS FOR HAND DRUMMING

1) Sitting Position:
Back Straight (space between back and chair)
Letter grade or a mark out of /10

2) Positioning the Drum:
Have the drum slanted away from your body (larger playing surface/allows the sound to escape)
Hold the drum in place with thighs
Use feet and ankles to hold the drum in place on the floor
Cross feet/ankles with smaller drums
Letter grade or a mark out of /10

3) Hand Position:
Create a triangle shape in the middle of your hands
Fingers should be together
Letter grade or a mark out of /10

4) Tone Production:
Hands are to "rebound" off the drum head (like bouncing a basketball)

Bass Tones = Middle of the Drum (FINGERS TOGETHER)

Open Tones = Edge of the drum (FINGERS TOGETHER, NO THUMBS)

Slap Tones = Edge of Drum (FINGERS SPREAD APART, SLAP the DRUM)

Letter grade or a mark out of /10

5) Participation:
Effort
On Task
Actively Participating
Musicality = Demonstrates an understanding of the musical concepts and applies them in a musical context
(Beat, Rhythm, Tempo, Dynamics)
Letter grade or a mark out of /10

THE SPIRIT OF WORLD DRUMMING TEST

40 marks

Name: _____

1. What is the proper **holding position** for larger types of hand drums? (3 marks)

2. What do you need to do differently when holding **smaller types** of hand drums? (1 mark)

3. What **position** do your hands and fingers need to be in when playing hand drums? (2 marks)

4. **Define** the following musical terms in your own words. (1 mark each)

Tempo / Beat / Rhythm / Dynamics

5. How do you **play** the following tones on the hand drum and what do these **African terms** stand for? (2 marks each)

Goon / Doon / Goe / Doe / Pah / Tah

6. Why do we need to keep the hand drum on an **angle** when playing on it? (2 marks)

7. The **Intro-Start Rhythm** that is played by the lead drummer in African forms of music has an important purpose. What are the two reasons that the drum leader starts of the song with an Intro - Start Rhythm? (2 marks)

8. What are the health benefits of participating in drum circles?
Essay format, 40 - 70 words, written in proper sentence/paragraph form. (14 marks)

<u>Choices:</u>   Senior Homes (social aspects)
               Hospitals (rehabilitation centre, social aspects and the physical benefits)
               Music Festivals
               School Music Programs (benefits of education)
               Group Homes

Drum Circle Fun for All Ages, "A Cross Cultural Music Program" Year at a Glance

Step #1

Introduction to various types of
DRUMS/PERCUSSION
Instruments from around the WORLD
*RESPECT of INSTRUMENTS &
EACH OTHER

Step #2

Positioning/Playing Hand Drums
-Sitting Position/Stay RELAXED
- Keep the drum in place, let the
sound escape from under the drum
- Hand Position: Create a Triangle
Shape in the middle of your hands

Step #3

Tone Production on Hand
Drums/Percussion Instruments
- Bass Tones (Goon/Doon)
- Open Tones (Goe/Doe)
-Slap Tones (Pah/Tah)
- Heel Toe (H/T)
- Fulcrom/Grip: Letting Drum
Stick(s)/Mallet(s) bounce

Step #4

MUSIC CONCEPTS
-Beat, Rhythm,
Textures, Dynamics,
Tempo, Time Signatures,
Staff,
Treble - Bass Clefs
* How do they work
together to create music?

Step #5

CREATING
MUSIC
Patterning
Time Signatures
Note Values
Rhythm Combinations
-Beat/Pulse/Tempo
-Reading Music Notation
Performing a variety forms of music
ECHO, CALL & RESPONSE,
MUSIC APPRECIATION,
COMMUNICATION,
LISTENING, ENSEMBLE ,
IMPROVISATION,
OSTINATO,
TEAM WORK,
Follow the DRUM
FACILITATOR

Step #6

Movement/Geography/Song/Culture & Society
- Where do these instruments, styles/forms of
music come from?
Maps, Listening Examples/Music Appreciation-Response Journals
-Sing songs, add movement with
drumming/songs

PERFORMING
School / Community / Nationally
ALL YEAR LONG
The Spirit of World Drumming

The Spirit of
WORLD DRUMMING

Presented to

_____

for demonstrating the SPIRIT of
WORLD DRUMMIMG
* Presented by
        Jeff Stewart,
            Your Drum Facilitator

RESOURCES FOR REFERENCE

The Soul of Hand Drumming
*by Doug Sole "**My Mentor**"*

The Art and Heart of Drum Circles
*by Christine Stevens "**My Mentor**"*

Drum Circle Spirit: Facilitating Human Potential through Rhythm
by Arthur Hull

Together in Rhythm/The Amazing Jamnasium
by Kalani my Guru

Latin-American Percussion: Rhythms and rhythm instruments from Cuba and Brazil
by Birger Sulsbruck

Drum Circle: A Guide to World Percussion
by Chalo Eduardo & Frank Kumor

World Music, A Cross - Cultural Curriculum
by Will Schmid

Songs of Ghana, Kpanlogo Songs
by Kwasi Dunyo

Conga Cookbook / Fundamentals of Latin Music for the Rhythm Section (DVD)
by Poncho Sanchez

Doumbec Delight
by Mary Ellen Donald

Bing Bang Boomwhackers, Volume 1
by Kevin Lepper, Anthony Gnuteck, Stacey Larson, Blake Wiener

Latin Sounds from the Drumset
by Frank "Chico" Guerrero

Brazilian Rhythms for Drumset
by Duduka Da Fonseca and Bob Weiner

Syncopation for the Modern Drummer
by Ted Reed

Stick Control for the Modern Drummer / Mallet Control for the Xylophone, Marimba, Vibraphone, Vibraharp
by George Lawrence Stone

A GUIDEBOOK for the MUSIC EDUCATOR
by Robert B. Breithaupt

World Music, The Rough Guide

Song Catchers, in search of the World's Music:
by Mickey Hart with K. M. Kostyal

DVDS / VIDEOS

Youssou N' Dour: Live in London / the world of Youssou N' Dour

Kodo, One Earth Tour Special

Buena Vista Social Club

STOMP OUT LOUD

Paul DeLong and Rick Gratton LIVE Video At Percussion Institute of Technology

Sting: Bring on the Night / Inside, The Songs of Sacred Love

Peter Gabriel: Secret World Live

RECORDS / TAPES / CDS

MUSIC AND RHYTHM, A BENEFIT LP FOR A WORLD OF MUSIC, ARTS AND DANCE

King Sunny Ade And His African Beats, "Juju Music"

SOUND D'AFRIQUE II 'SOUKOUS'

SWEET ELIZABETH: A. B. Crentsil with Eric Agyemang

DOLLAR BRAND: Abdullah Ibrahim

Babatunde Olatunji: Drums of Passion / Circle of Drums

THE BEST OF AFRICA 20th CENTURY MASTERS: The Millennium Collection

THE RHYTHMATIST: STEWART COPELAND

WORLD MUSIC NETWORK PRESENTS: THE ROUGH GUIDE TO WORLD MUSIC

AIRTO MOREIRA: Struck By Lightning

THE MONDO MELODIA SERIIES: MONDO SAMBA

PUTUMATA PRESENTS: BRAZILIAN GROOVE

Titi Puente: PARTY WITH PUENTE!

Jane Bunnett: Alma De Santiago

THE SPIRIT OF CUBA - Hilario Duran

Hossam Ramzy: The Best of Volume #1 & #2

BELLY dance INSTRUMENTALS from Morocco and Lebanon

Ryuichi Sakamoto: Thousand Knives / NEO GEO / Merry Christmas Mr. Lawrence

JEFF STEWART

Remo Endorsed Drum Circle Facilitator/Vic Firth Endorsed

My Bliss is to devote my life to facilitating Drum Circles.

Currently Jeff is facilitating "The Spirit of World Drumming Circles" and share the Spirit & Health of Drumming. He is also a keynote speaker promoting community through drumming for music educators and drumming enthusiasts of all ages.

Jeff is a dedicated educator who facilitates drum circles in his community and at various music festivals, such as the Northern Lights Festival, Summerfest, Sault Ste Marie Echoes Drum Festival, Celtic Fest, Muhtadi International Drum Festival, Calgary International Reggae Fest. He has also facilitated drum circles and clinics for the Rainbow Public & Catholic School Boards, Laurentian Hospital Rehab Center, Laurentian University Music/Education/International Student Association, ICAN, Crisis Intervention Annual Conference, AIDS Awareness Conference, Mental Health Awareness, International Science Center Conference and at the Ontario Music Educators Association Conferences.

In July of 2005 Jeff also had the pleasure of facilitating "The Spirit of World Drumming" for participants from all around the World at the **XV World Transplant Games** held in London, Ontario.

Jeff's **Sudbury World Community Drum Circle** performed as the opening act for the **CTV Lion's Club Children's Christmas Telethon** (Live Television). They have also performed at **Cancer Relay Walk for Life, Science North Canada Day, Dragon Boat Races, Drum Corps International (dci) "Spectacle for Sound", Organ Donor Awareness, Shave for the Cure for Cancer Research, Earth Day** and have been the opening act for **Latin Bands** playing concerts at the Caruso Club and Respect is Burning.

Freelance Work

Besides being a prominent music educator and clinician, Jeff also performs professionally. For the past 12 years Jeff has led his own jazz ensemble "**Solar Jazz Ensemble**". This group has performed at various functions and music festivals. Jeff has also been the primary drummer/percussionist for the **Mauricio Montecinos Latin Band** and has performed at a variety of music festivals in Ontario, CBC live radio and television sessions. Since 1994 Jeff has performed on live television for the **CTV Lions Club Telethon** as permanent percussionist in the house band. He has independently been writing/recording a wide variety of world international forms of music.

Education
Bachelor of Education, Nipissing University
Bachelor of Arts, Major: Music (percussion/jazz) Laurentian University
Humber College of Applied Arts, Music Performance (percussion major)
Village Music Circles Certified Drum Circle Facilitator

Jeff Stewart has also studied privately with legendary drummers/percussionists such as Doug Sole-Soul Drums (Drum Circle mentor 2002-present), Christine Stevens-UpBeat Drums (Drum Circle mentor), Famoudoa Konate, Saikou Sahou, Paul DeLong, Rick Gratton, Memo Acevedo (currently teaching at New York University of Music), Roger Flock and Don Vickery (Humber College), Jack Broumpton (Laurentian University), Tony Azzopardi, Rick Lazar (Montuno Police, The Samba Squad, Toronto), Ed Thigpen (Oscar Peterson, Oliver Jones), Arthur Hull (Pioneer of community drum circles), Kalani (DCM).

A PERSONAL REFLECTION

* The Spirit of DRUMMING
is the SOUL of LIFE
* Let your RHYTHM
Guide you to a Positive LIFE!